WHEN A DONUT GOES TO THERAPY

Copyright © 2021 Erin Winters

All rights reserved.
No part of this publication may be reproduced or distributed in any form without prior written consent from the publisher.

Illustrations and cover design by Kaitin Bucher

Hardback ISBN: 978-1-7343464-6-6
Paperback ISBN: 978-1-7343464-7-3

SNOWFALL
PUBLICATIONS LLC

Special Thanks
Kib and Lily Pearson
The Wilkins Family
Rachel E. Holz

To the brave people doing the hard work of therapy.

Thank you to Wyndhurst Counseling Center and Wellness for your support of this project and dedication to the mental health care of the Lynchburg, VA community!

www.wyndhurstcounselingcenter.com

When a donut goes to therapy,
at first he feels all **nervous.**
He does not know what it is like
to have this kind of service.

Inside he feels all quivery,
a shake within his belly.
He does not know what to expect.
His stomach turns to **jelly!**

The donut walks back to a room he thought would feel so **stuffy.** Surprised, he finds a play box with some toys and Bunny Fluffy.

The sand box sitting on the shelf
is filled with **figurines,**
and Donut is allowed to play
with puppets, by all means!

They draw and play and talk on days that Donut feels he wants to. He **cries,** he **laughs,** and sometimes has what people call a **breakthrough.**

When a donut goes to therapy,
he starts to understand
That it's **okay** to feel dismay
and take a helping hand.

At first he thought his feelings were
too big and he was worried,
but change that lasts is made of work
and rarely is it hurried.

When a donut goes to therapy,
he feels some big **emotions**.
He learns to **breathe** in like a wave
and out back to the oceans.

Then one day, the donut trusts the therapist enough to **bravely face** what's in the dark, the deep and scary stuff.

He talks about the **monster** that is hiding in his room, the **hurt** and **pain** that happen there, the great impending doom.

He says that he is feeling rather
empty in the middle.
He really wants to feel fulfilled
if even just a little.

The donut draws a **secret** with a paper and a pen. It helps the donut to feel **safer** every now and then.

When a donut goes to therapy,
he has a **helping team**,
a superhero's sidekick friends,
like sprinkles on whipped cream.

The hero and his super team will **fight** to save the day from nightmares and from dangers 'til the scary goes away.

The donut also learns to draw
his **big** and **little** mad.
He learns that when he squeezes Fluff,
he feels a little glad.

He is **wise** because he knows
that feeling feelings isn't bad.
He is **strong** because he knows
just what to do when he feels sad.

- 5 JUMPING JACKS
- 10 DEEP BREATHS
- SQUEEZE FISTS FOR 10 SECONDS
- SPIN IN A CIRCLE

When a donut ends his therapy,
he's **proud** of what he's done.
It's a warm and joyful feeling
that's like sitting in the sun.

He gives high-fives to his old teammate,
confident once more
that he can handle hard life things,
no matter what's in store!

FOR KIDS

What is therapy?
Going to therapy doesn't mean there is anything wrong with you.
Therapists are adults that want to help you feel safe and happy,
just like doctors, but they don't give you any shots. Therapy is for
playing, drawing, and talking about anything big that happens
in your life, good or bad.
What kinds of things do you think Donut might have gone to therapy for?

What does Donut do in therapy?
Donut talks when he wants to, but he doesn't have to.
Donut can draw and play! What is your favorite thing to play?

Do you tell my parents everything I tell you?
Ask your therapist! Typically, no. If you want your parents to know something,
we will definitely tell them! Sometimes parents need to know a little bit about
what is going on, and other times it is okay not to share things you don't
want to share. The most important thing is that you feel comfortable and
are safe, and learn about emotions and what to do when you feel them.
What do you wish your parents knew about you?
Is there anything you don't want them to know?

How often does someone go to therapy?
It depends! Sometimes as much as several times a week, and
other times only once a week or every other week.

Donut has a superhero helping team to encourage and support him!
Who is on your support team? Who are the safe adults in your life?

**What happens to the size of the hole in Donut's middle from the beginning of
the book to the end? Why do you think it changes?**
Therapy doesn't solve all of our problems, but it can make them feel less scary
and not so big, and help us know what to do to feel better!

FOR ADULTS

Why choose play therapy over traditional talk therapy?
Play therapy is an evidence based treatment for most presenting concerns that helps children process in their language — PLAY. Kids process their world differently than adults do, and this approach engages them where they are in a meaningful, effective way. The truth is that we can process in different ways, and though kids certainly do often talk in therapy, the pressure is off and they don't have to.

If you ask what your child did in therapy and they said play, that's what you want!
Play can be more strategic, scientific, and effective than just talking, so in the hands of a licensed professional, play is a powerful tool... and kids are more likely to want to come!

Can I sit in?
Sometimes, yes. Day to day, typically no. Therapy for kids works best when the family is supportive and involved, and especially during the intake, this is important. Family sessions all together are also beneficial. At the same time, the therapist needs room to establish a positive, safe relationship with the child so that they feel comfortable opening up. Ask the therapist questions about their process early on!

Can you tell me what they share in session?
It is often best for parents not to ask the therapist for specifics on the session content, to allow the child to feel they are truly free to share whatever they like. Feel free to ask for general progress updates, observe differences at home, or consider a family session to talk all together about how it's going. Age and situation vary, so ASK!

How can I best support a child in therapy?
Be there for them and create a safe, unconditionally loving atmosphere. If the child is comfortable, you can ask open-ended questions about how therapy is going, and when the child shares, validate their experiences and offer support as needed.

NAME YOUR FEELINGS

What are you feeling right now? If you aren't sure, flip through the book. Can you see a time when Donut felt the way you feel now? Point to the emotion and ask a safe adult to help you learn its name. It might also be helpful To look at a feelings chart to learn to name more emotions!

TELL ABOUT YOUR FEELINGS

Once you know what the emotion is that you are feeling, describe what it is like for you to have inside.
Tell about a time you felt nervous, sad, angry, or excited. What did it make you want to do? What did you choose to do?

FEEL YOUR FEELINGS

Draw an outline of a person, or ask a safe adult to help you. Color in red the parts of your body you notice when you feel angry. Does your face get hot, your hands sweaty, or your chest feel tight? Color in blue the parts of your body you notice when you feel sad. Do you feel a lump in your throat, or tears on your face?

It's okay to feel your feelings! That's exactly what helps them get free - feeling them, describing and acknowledging them, and letting them go.

MANAGE YOUR FEELINGS

Emotions aren't good or bad...they just are! It's what we choose to do when we feel emotions that is most important. It's okay to feel sad or mad, but hurting ourselves or someone else, running into the street, and breaking things aren't healthy or safe ways to feel our feelings. Instead, maybe we can count to 10, take deep breaths, or talk to a safe person.

Donut makes a list of coping skills toward the end of the book. Can you make a list of coping skills that might help you feel your feelings in a positive and safe way?

EMOTIONS SAVE THE DAY

Sometimes emotions aren't fun to feel, and it's easy to think the ones we don't like aren't important. In reality, each emotion has been created for a purpose, to keep you and the world around you safe and healthy.

JOY
Joy is an emotion we love to feel! It feels safe and happy, content, and peaceful. Joy tells us that something in our world is safe and good, and we can relax and enjoy it.

FEAR
Fear warns us when something is unsafe, and keeps us from making dangerous decisions. If we really want to get a toy that fell into the deep end of the pool, but we don't know how to swim, the fear of being in the deep water will remind us we should stop what we are doing and ask a safe adult for help! If a person makes us feel afraid, we can talk to someone we trust about it.

SADNESS
Sadness helps our brain process hard things that happen to us, grieve to honor a deep struggle or person we love, and have empathy for other people in their pain. Sadness helps us to connect with other people in deep ways and to think about things that are not okay in our world.

ANGER
Anger is like a waving red flag telling us something is wrong in our world and making us want to change situations that are unjust or unfair. Sometimes being sad helps us process what is happening, but anger or frustration is what motivates us to do something about it!

ABOUT THE AUTHOR

Erin Winters is a Licensed Professional Counselor, mom, and founder of Snowfall Publications LLC. Erin uses her clinical knowledge and experience to write high quality therapeutic children's books normalizing emotions and promoting mental health.

Erin has worked in a variety of mental health settings including a child and adolescent psychiatric unit at a hospital, intensive in-home therapy, substance abuse programs for adults, and currently works in an outpatient setting with a variety of client ages, struggles, and goals.

When she isn't working or writing, Erin loves spending time with her husband and their two little boys, reading novels, and drinking hot chocolate.

LEARN MORE